Susquehanna Quarters

Kevin Cawley

Glass Darkly

2012

These poems appeared in the Susquehanna Quarterly between Spring 1999 and Winter 2002.Wiley Clements selected them.

ISBN: 978-1-300-34736-1

Brown Wolf

Does it matter in the story of a dog
if only the dog has character, if humans
behave as fatefully as weather systems?
The dog rejects their California doctrine,

chews his rope and strikes out for the Klondike.
Again and again the tag around his neck
delivers him in a cage to their discretion.
They make him sleep indoors. He howls at night.

At last they let him choose, and for a while
he chooses to remain. But in the end
he hears the call again, and California

fails to overcome it. With a most
apologetic look he moves along,
chews his ties and strikes out for the north.

Darkening Ages

An overlay of surface dirt obscures
paintings in oil, Baroque and Renaissance.
Typical, how dinginess endures
beyond the term of light -- how all our wants

however bright they look will turn the corner
down this alley brown with lowering grime.
And yet from evidence like this we garner
authoritative summaries of time.

Considering my particular bazaar
I can't imagine how it used to look --
billowy silks, lamps gaudier than gold.

Centuries of Brownian motion mar
perception so discreetly I mistook
these new lamps on the peddler's cart for old.

The Walk

Flame in the tree-top:
lame on the tongue
talk never touches what
walking discovers.

Leaves gone to red-orange
grieve at the frost:
words only fracture what
birds fly away from.

Ice on the ditch-water:
nice cloud of vapor
flies from the mouth as it
tries to describe it.

Crow in the tree-top
knows not to bother:
caws to the walker what
laws please a lizard.

Stop Action

A spider web with coats of frost
providing extra emphasis
hangs like macrame across
the corner of the shed. And this

delectable inconsequence,
at large when practicality
declines, calls up uncommon sense.
Which looks a while. And lets things be.

The Misfortune of Having Missed out on Pessimism

A man sits in the Cleveland Public Library.
He never heard of Schopenhauer. Marble
banisters guide him when he climbs the stairs.
But usually he takes the elevator.
This afternoon he reads a mystery.
The grey that passes for sunshine in that region
gives way to the grey that passes for twilight. Pigeons
in grey plumage pay no attention to tourists.
Sightseers wait for a bus and watch the pigeons,
having nothing better to do at the moment.
Later they plan to visit Garfield's tomb.
Earlier they toured the Public Library,
the largest in the country to allow
the poor to wander through its open stacks.
Therefore the man could someday possibly
happen upon Spinoza. Schopenhauer,
mentioned on page nineteen of the mystery,
has made no great impression. Nevertheless,
no longer can we class the man as one
who never heard of Schopenhauer. Instead
we must content ourselves to say: He never
studied Spinoza, though someday he might.

Ongoing

Rust flakes off the maple tree
cover half our Autumn lawn
Summer having come and gone
without the slightest help from me.

Preoccupied with marriage plans
I look at flowers sold in stores
not at blooming weeds outdoors.
I drink my colors out of cans.

Nature nevertheless occurs
no matter what occurs to me.
Rust flakes off the maple tree.
Squirrels grow their winter furs.

Bleach

Wife of one day
she bleached his grey socks.
She washed her own watch.
What will he say?

He's taken the batteries
out of her clocks.
He's never used bleach.
(He says, "what's the matter?")

Not even on whites.
He seldom locks locks.
He hates ticking clocks.
They haven't had fights

but they do disagree.
(She says, "Come and see.")
Married one day.
What will he say?

A Preference in Weather

However thick-headed it makes me feel,
I have nothing against drizzle: I rather enjoy
gloom in the skylight, runnels, drops
in progress down a sloping glass.
This animation of the glaze
promises and delivers change:
small change accumulating makes
for major currency. The window's
shedding freshets now. I breathe
relief, unfurl my folded gills.
I've had my gasp of brilliance
in the dry domain of men:
my attic's under water;
I'm amphibious again.

The Big Idea

Whats have roots and branches
tendrils cracking fire:
an earth composed of answers
invites them to inquire.

Downward, outward, upward
they split rock, split the sky:
lapping up their supper
they push away the why.

De Light

The middle of nowhere's somewhere once
a body builds a cabin there:
wrapped up in light, delighted under
late October maples, I
interrogate enlightenment:
here the roads have potholes: rain
has made them all reflecting pools:
the literal-minded take my point:
light overhead, light underfoot,
left, right, left: ahead, behind:
an easy yoke, my burden light:
response ability in sight.

Super Market

Rose moon at sundown
me with my groceries
taking a breather
finding it strange:
round as the coin
in my pocket, token
hardly worth carrying,
eunuch of change.

Change keeps coming
valued or not
the moon waxes
the moon wanes
once in a while
the moon wears rouge
and gleans a few glances
for all her pains.

Rip

Pulled over by the littoral
my figurative bent
catches a rip that takes me out
beyond the currency of route
beyond the beggary of gulls
into the deeply meant.

The best advice from those ashore
says never to resist
but ride it out beyond the bar
where currents end and chances are
the best can make it back to shore --
where chances are the best.

Those who try to swim against
the current always drown:
the strongest swimmers end up dead --
they stroke but fail to get ahead,
their headstrong lifeguards' confidence
too dense to come around.

Robert Forst

Preposterous thing to do with a pen --
signing my name again and again
until I fumble and get it wrong:
the fallible hand that framed the song
numb with a dream that cramps its style.
A while to go? Too long a while.

What mockery of original thought --
so much admired it has me caught
mired in a repetitious act
writing reduced to meaningless fact
the spelling of my taken name
always or almost always the same.

And what will they do with the one mistake?
One of a kind. Wouldn't it make
an autograph vampire lust even more
quiver to own at the quisling core
this bug this antigen of song
stupidly written and written wrong?

Beyond Rubies

I never wear apparel
and hardly ever pose
in anything as daring
as negligee or hose.

Because the gate is narrow
and nosy heaven knows
I never wear apparel
just ordinary clothes.

Fly Paper

Why we call a fly-leaf
what we call it I can't say:
a moment ago an insect
landed on this trap
which had no glue to hold it.

Nor does it hold me.
So I turn the page and study
more attractive tracts.
But do the phrases stick
or do I stick to them?

Flies immobilized
on the paper in my brain
wiggle a while and die:
or I myself a fly
walking a tacky way.

Lounge

A long chaise in the sunroom would do nicely;
furnish it the way you would the lawn.
I'll sit there in the morning with my coffee.

In winter, when its draftiness betrays
the inefficiency of single windows
I'll wrap my feet in blankets -- and my shoulders.

I like the way the floor creaks when I walk.
I feel the give flow through me, sole to scalp.
I like the coloration of the carpet.

Once a monotonous solid, it faded, bled,
succumbed to floods and sunlight, wore away
a pattern, record of its mammal's habits.

The old mock torso and its pedestal
can stay. Perhaps I'll make my friend a dress.
I've always liked the company of scarecrows.

Stalling

All those years I wore
no footwear whatsoever:
barefoot in the shower!
But now I've promised never
to jog another stall
without my running shoes
to keep me on my toes.
The fallen pay their dues.
Nevertheless in time
I'll falter and repeat
my unoriginal trope,
trippingly tongue defeat.

Lobster Subservient

To comfort a lobster
one has to get wet;
she does not in fact
make a very good pet.

Won't come when you call her,
won't beg or play dead,
won't purr when you pet her
or mew to get fed.

You want an admirer,
want to play god --
a creature to worship you,
give you the nod.

Lobster won't go for it.
Lacking a head,
best she can manage:
get boiled, turn red.

Focus

We pray continually as commanded
by the force of Natural Law. We can't
pause for a moment. Every gripe goes up
to heaven like a helium balloon.
Every yelp of pleasure, every curse
courses away. Concentric waves of will
rebound from every pebble we release
until a formless turbulence prevails.

Occasionally an individual learns
to calm that surface, still that stormy business,
throw over all throwing over for a while.
Imagine a pond flat as a plate glass table:
the child above it listens for a moment,
leans on a balanced boulder, tips it in.

100% Natural

Geese go their way, I go mine.
Prattle about the Natural
preoccupies the party line
my children use to shoot the bull.

Out the window as I wait
impatient for the phone to clear
a flock of Canadas in flight
points out the flaw in what I hear.

Their honking made me think of hounds
about to tree a trite raccoon --
associating sight and sound
I catch them as they cross the moon.

With Nature's creatures in the dark
beyond a barrier of glass
we tell each other how things work
and miss them when they come to pass.

Reluctance

The way a cat will linger at the door
pace and scratch until you open it
and let the night air nip, the way a cat
will linger there as you impatiently

nudge her with your toe, the way a cat
will hump up like a caterpillar then,
walk halfway out and all the way back in,
the way a cat will linger at the door

reminds me of myself in my approach
to evening and its promises, my wad
fattening the wallet in my pocket,

wealth to an uncomfortable degree --
and I with plans to dance and do some drinking
logy-legged pause inside the door.

Tribute

Beauty in uniform, Truth in drag,
and Good in a hooded monastic rag
appeared at my door one Halloween,
the oldest children I'd ever seen.

I knew if I told them to go away
they'd make me sick with the tricks they'd play,
but since I consented to pay their tax
they thanked me blankly and turned their backs.

The Difference of Indifference

Nature does not disdain as we do.
It likes brown leaves as well as green.
It has no word for weed or freedom.
We can't say what its signals mean.

We sense its contradictions, given
opposites by which we live.
Denials of death by which we're driven
know it in the negative.

Death does not dismay it: lively
dialectic to survive
depends on death, on strife, on striving
mortals deadly while alive.

Placid as dust around a seed
through drought and storm, in brown and green,
it writes a weed: to call it freedom
dwells on what it doesn't mean.

Photons for an Exhibition

Spun honey spread
on whole grain bread

the lawn alive
with mourning doves

birds the grey
of shaley scree

an undertone
of bygone green

and leaves the shade
of unstained wood

half overhead
half of them spread

from picket fence
to picket fence

a gloss as bland
as common sense.

My kitchen window
takes it in

the fence, the shed
square in its grid

boxes around
bright boughs, bright ground

a patch of mind
a camera blind

squares of color
standing still

squares of time
in wooden frames

reflections passing
panes of glass

already missing
what they've passed.

Pigs

We people corrupted the pigs.
They never used to wallow.
The wild boar, a fellow
careful of his digs,

had dignity to bristle,
wit to take offense,
muscle fit to tense
tough tendon, able gristle.

A fat man whose disaster
has taught him to grow lean
and shrunk his clothing clean
has studied with a master.

And pigs that get away
run grunting through the woods
deprived of earthly goods
but given back to play.

Aunt Alien

Family faces in a baby's face
framed in an heirloom spiderweb of lace,
genes of immigrants in dingy ships
apparent in a parody of lips,

wrinkle of rage, angle of angry chin,
complexion more than texture of the skin
declaring independence as if cast
in plastic from some sculpture of the past:

an icon of implicit criticism
amalgamating in a human prism
elders with their disapproving glares,

their appetites, their petty princely airs,
and something else, a well-remembered grin --
Aunt Alien when she called the children in.

Vapor

I pour myself a bowl of steam,
vapor to clear the phlegm away.
The word translated vanity,
the Hebrew word Ecclesiastes
uses, means more literally

vapor, breath, the smoke a mouth
expresses in the winter air.
Not bad at all: we all need breath
and moisture in the mix of ether,
vapor not too dry to breathe.

It comes to pass: the fate of steam
inevitably to drift away --
dissolve, disintegrate, as we,
like personalities of gas,
dissolve ourselves in going free.

Devil's Food

Giving your devils their due
we nevertheless observe
the bone chips in their gluey stew,
their nourishment of nerve.

Have they a right to eat?
Enlightened appetite
finds brain and testicle both sweet,
likes cheese gone blue with blight.

Human brains taste best.
Human testicles
make oysters that surpass the rest
and pickle well in dill.

You advocates must find us
narrow-minded, dense.
You say they want to serve mankind.
We wonder in what sense.

On Meeting Adam in the Afterlife

We mumble and seem somewhat hard of hearing.
Whatever you've been saying, I say "What?"
Whatever I've been saying, you say "Pardon?"
Bodily limitations undercut
the wit we might no longer need to mutter
if Michael let us burgle Adam's garden.

If Adam met us in the afterlife
how well would we communicate? What English
could a couple on the ball, never
so much the souls of wit as now, our tongues
turned into flame, our speech made into song,
employ with one who found himself too clever?

Enlightenment

At 13 months my daughter
took notice of the birds
lighting on their feeder.
At a loss for words

she pointed at them, made her
noises of delight.
She didn't have their number:
she couldn't count to eight.

Uncountable and nameless,
a tale she'd never tell:
the melting veil of sameness,
a woman at the well.

Free Fall

Tree-borne trash has now completely
tarred and feathered my dead car:
all organic, healthy fallout,
maple-scrap adhesive tape,
glops of pasty rock-dove dropping,
storm-wrack twigs that scratch and scar.

Inert for half a year. A certain
seasonable dignity
accumulates in time, a rumor
of November. And I love
the solitude implied by fall,
with me on foot and far from company.

Success requires engines, vessels,
single-minded voyagings.
Failure lets a person bail
out. Fall free. I have no doubt
achieved a failure here -- by leaving
things alone to do their things.

Tempted, sometimes, to attempt
to charge the battery and start
the motor just to hear it go,
I settle for some running water,
a nuzzle with a hose nozzle.
My garden ornament, my work of art.

Religious Perspectives

Heisenberg imagined he had found
a final answer in uncertainty,
boasted on a book jacket sounding
more pedantic than some parody.

Heidegger complained that we are still
not thinking; his most thought-provoking thought
implied however that our children will
because they will have savored what he taught.

I knew a man with cancer who had read
both Heisenberg and Heidegger. He died
before the age of forty in a bed
surrounded by the scripture he denied.

He'd made his living criticizing critics.
Dying made him cranky. Over tea
he taught his seminar the place of pity.
Superstition. Ancient history.

from **Father of Pearl**

One might suppose the animals
would shy away from human trails
test the oddly stunted tracks
pause to nose them, smell the smells.

The rabbit I imagine here
inhabiting this patch of trees
would vanish in the undergrowth
renounce the human dream of ease.

A path made broad by traffic, flat
by athletes on their morning run
made white by freshly fallen snow --
and I arrive before the sun

to walk it in my gum-soled shoes,
to walk to work, the same old news.
But look! Fresh tracks of rabbit show
one took the way I mean to go.

*   *   *   *

The window by my desk at work
makes splendid days look bleak to me:
a milky way between the panes
welcomes the milky way I see.

Eyes that make for life-long fog
try to peer through cloudy glass,
inhale a cloudless afternoon
through veils of vapor, solid gas.

But as the afternoon wears on
by passing down and out the sun
enters the purview of my panes
to interview me one on one.

Blinded by this repartee
blindly I begin to say
I see. Because of course I don't.
But feel I might now, not I won't.

*   *   *   *

When solitude involves a soul,
hollow full of hollow, how
can loneliness solidify?
Only an empty question now.

Appointments having lead to dis-
appointments, as they often do,
alone means loneliness again,
a bone to gnaw, a haunting Who?

* * * *

A rosary of resentments: as
she dozes in bed she tells her beads,
ticks off the things that tick her off
plucking them out like garden weeds.

A psychological device
making religion obsolete.
As Cupid to her Psyche once
(how stupid) I agreed to meet.

A marriage of impediments.
Carefully we kept things dark,
shut bushel baskets, loads of light,
put curiosity in park.

But thanks to the lamp of therapy
(thank God) she got the best of me:
they frightened her, peculiar things,
my light, my easy yoke of wings.

www.ingramcontent.com/pod-product-compliance
Ingram Content Group UK Ltd.
Pitfield, Milton Keynes, MK11 3LW, UK
UKHW041903190726
13854UKWH00003B/1057

9 781300 347361